I0457673

THE TREASURE HUNT

A GUIDE TO MAXIMIZING WEALTH

BY CHARISSA TURNBULL

www.inomniaparatuspublishing.com

BEFORE WE EMBARK

Hello and welcome to the first steps in your next money Journey! I am so excited to have you here and so grateful that you have chosen me as your guide! We are going to go on an amazing journey together, but first let me introduce myself and get a few housekeeping things out of the way!

I am Charissa Turnbull (Sha-REE-Sa if you were wondering), an intuitive financial coach, real estate expert, published author and all around wealth builder! I believe wholeheartedly in creating a no judgment zone to talk about, celebrate, grow and build wealth while living our dream lives at the same time! Part of our human experience gets to be about living life as we see fit, it gets to be about whatever we want.

Impact. Expansion. Fun. Adventure. Generosity.

Anything and everything - that is the point, YOU get to decide!

So many of us have challenging money pasts and so much obligation built around the people we love that it can be difficult to allow things to just flow, including our money.

Building wealth while simultaneously living our dream lives requires spending money in alignment with these things, but that can be hard and scary.

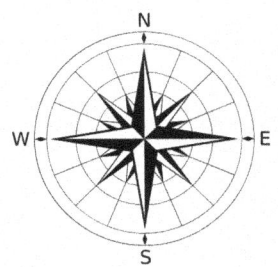

WELCOME ABOARD

In The Treasure Hunt we are going to work through a few concepts that sometimes hold even the smartest and most successful people back from living in full alignment while building serious amounts of wealth.

At the end of this journal we will have put words and understanding to your relationship with money, allowing you to really develop it into one of abundance and excitement.

We will have analyzed, mapped and broken down your money story in its entirety allowing you to heal and shift anything that is no longer serving you.

In chapter 3 we will be breaking down things that trigger unwanted spending and saving patterns and have built a system to provide a guiding light as these things happen in the future.

At the end of it all we will have an opportunity to reflect on everything you have learned about yourself and really decide what is next.

A few quick thoughts before we dive in:

This journal is exactly that, a journal, it is an opportunity for you to capture your thoughts around money and life and really look deep into yourself to find the reasons why you do certain things and feel certain ways about things.

It works best the more honest you are so many of the prompts will be free write style where I ask you t o "brain dump" around an idea. The less you censor yourself the more your higher self will come through and show you what you need to see.
I am so excited for you to embrace this journey of self discovery, self love and so much self permission!

-Charissa

CHAPTER ONE

UNDERSTANDING YOUR PERSONAL REALTIONSHIP WITH MONEY

There is no need for stress, fear or guilt where money is concerned, or with anything, really, so we are going to do some exercises to make it easier to focus on letting those things go and making decisions based on happiness and joy!

Of course I understand that this can be easier said than done, or at least feel that way. The first step to letting these things go is to understand where they come from and how you have built your relationship with money around them.

The magic, the key to the treasure chest so to speak, is always found in understanding the "why" around not just our behaviors but the stories we tell ourselves. We will dive more into this in chapter 2 but for now think about the following questions:

How do you feel about money?
I love it!
I like it fine but it isn't really part of my day to day thoughts.
I am indifferent towards it.
I hate it and actively avoid talking about or thinking about it.

Whichever one you have chosen, do you always feel that way about money? What about the things money either allows or doesn't allow you to have?

Now, set a timer for 10 minutes and free write about all the reasons you think you feel this way. If you feel all of these things at different times, that is ok too, write about all of them. Try not to censor yourself and just write out every thought that comes into your mind. There is no structure required, you may even go on a tangent about something that feels unrelated, just keep writing and let it flow.

Set your timer and explore your thoughts

_____
_____
_____
_____
_____
_____
_____
_____
_____
_____
_____
_____
_____
_____
_____
_____
_____
_____
_____
_____
_____
_____
_____
_____
_____
_____
_____
_____
_____
_____
_____
_____
_____

Take a few minutes and reread what you wrote. What conclusions can you make from your thoughts around the way you think and feel about money? Are there opportunities to make a shift?

_____
_____
_____
_____
_____
_____
_____
_____
_____
_____
_____
_____
_____
_____
_____
_____
_____
_____
_____
_____
_____
_____
_____
_____
_____
_____
_____

CHAPTER TWO

ANALYZING YOUR MONEY STORY

In the first chapter we started to break down some reasons why your relationship with money is what it is. It is important to note that even if you have an amazing relationship with money it is good to know why. Understanding the "why" will help you determine the best ways to build and maintain your wealth in both the short and the long term.

In this Chapter we are going to map out your money story in its entirety. A money story is simply everything that has happened in your life up until today that has shaped and influenced the way you think and feel about money.

This chapter includes 21 journal prompts. I recommend doing one prompt daily for 21 days. If you choose to work ahead, give yourself an opportunity to read and reflect on the previous prompt before moving on.

Describe in detail the first time you recognized what money was. Even if you didn't completely understand it.

How old were you?
What were you doing?
Describe the scene in detail.
Who was with you?
What time of year was it?

You get the idea! Describe everything that was physically present, as much as you are able. Really allow your memory to reflect and connect to your younger self. It sometimes helps to go into a meditative state. Take your time in the visualization process.

As you do this, really feel it. How do you feel about the situation? Avoid using terms like good or bad / positive / negative. Be as detailed as possible.

_____
_____
_____
_____
_____
_____
_____
_____
_____
_____
_____
_____
_____
_____
_____
_____
_____
_____
_____
_____
_____

Day Two

Think back to yesterday's memory and journal on the following questions:

What did I learn from this experience?
Do I have other memories that have reinforced these learnings?

NOTE: It is important to allow your mind to go deep here. Ask your higher self for guidance and trust your intuition. Nobody knows you better than you. Allow yourself to be guided by your past, present and future self.

_____
_____
_____
_____
_____
_____
_____
_____
_____
_____
_____
_____
_____
_____
_____
_____
_____
_____
_____
_____
_____
_____
_____
_____
_____

Day Three

Today we are going to do the same prompts from Day 2 but with a fresh mind and new perspective.

Ask yourself, what else? What else can "present you" learn from this past experience and the learnings you took from it?

How is this still influencing you today?

_____
_____
_____
_____
_____
_____
_____
_____
_____
_____
_____
_____
_____
_____
_____
_____
_____
_____
_____
_____
_____
_____
_____

Day Four

Do the learnings from this experience support your dream life?
Do you want to keep them?
Why?

Give 3-5 examples on how you can use these learnings to support your dream life and the same on how it does not. Remember, there are 2 sides to every coin. There is serve and limit in every action, memory and lesson.

_____
_____
_____
_____
_____
_____
_____
_____
_____
_____
_____
_____
_____
_____
_____
_____
_____
_____
_____
_____
_____
_____
_____
_____
_____
_____
_____
_____
_____
_____

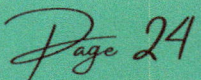

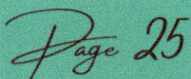

Day Five

Time to shift to something else for a few days!

Describe your relationship with money. Describe it as if it is a romantic partner.

Is it loving and supportive? Toxic, codependent? Maybe it is a little bit of all of them. This is another exercise where you are encouraged to free write. Allow all of your thoughts to come through. No censorship. It doesn't matter if it feels relevant or not. If it comes to mind, write it out until you have nothing left

_____

_____

_____

_____

_____

_____

_____

_____

_____

_____

_____

_____

_____

_____

_____

_____

_____

_____

_____

_____

_____

_____

_____

_____

_____

Day Six

Another free writing exercise. Read all the questions below at least twice before you start. Take five minutes to really let them absorb and read them again, then begin to write.

It is important to follow the process listed above. Allow your mind to really absorb. Consider memories, consider goals and consider who you are before you answer.

How do you feel about how you spend, save and invest? How do you decide on these things? How much of the money you spend directly supports the life you want to live? How do you feel about that number. If you could wave a magic wand and change something about the way you spend and save - taking all the effort out of it would you? What would you change?

_____
_____
_____
_____
_____
_____
_____
_____
_____
_____
_____
_____
_____
_____
_____
_____
_____
_____
_____
_____
_____
_____

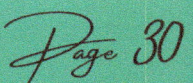

Day Seven

Starting at Day 1 reread all of your entries. At the end of each one, take the time to add any additional notes that you see fit.

Now that you have done so, write about the connection of each individual entry to each other entry. How has that money memory influenced your past and present habits? How have the memory and your habits influenced how you feel about money, your relationship, etc.? Really take the time to find the connections. You may need to read the past entries more than once.

_____
_____
_____
_____
_____
_____
_____
_____
_____
_____
_____
_____
_____
_____
_____
_____
_____
_____
_____
_____
_____
_____
_____
_____
_____
_____
_____

List out 25 money beliefs you have, or that have been told to you.

Example: Rich people are selfish, Mo' Money Mo' Problems, Money changes you, I work hard for my money...

Good, bad or otherwise just write them out. If you have more than 25 that is fine but you need at least 25. These don't have to be all things you believe. It could be just a philosophy you heard. The idea is to capture as many money beliefs from your environment and life up until now.

Day Nine

Read your list from yesterday. Do you have anything to add?

Now, go through and circle any of them that you believe – even just a little.

On a new sheet of paper rewrite all of the beliefs that you hold to be true, then number them a 1, 2, or 3:

1. I want to keep this belief.
2. I want to let this belief go.
3. I am not sure.

Try not to use 3 unless you can write out the benefits of both sides of the belief.

Finally, Do a quick Google search of "Positive Money Beliefs"

Go through and fill in how ever many you need to build your list back to 25 money beliefs that you WANT to keep. No repeats, and only pick ones that truly resonate. If you are having a hard time coming up with 25, leave it and come back to it. It is important that all of these resonate with you, your life, and your goals.

This time it is less important that you actually believe them, but they all need to be things you want to believe.

Write them all out and add anything with a 3 at the bottom (these don't count to towards the 25).

Day Ten

Today is going to be all about understanding your money beliefs and how they influence you. Read through your final list from Day 9 and come up with 5 overall feeling themes for the entire list.

Journal on the following questions:

Is there a primary theme about my money beliefs?

What is the significance of this theme in my life?

Where else can I see this theme?

How does this theme make me feel?

For all the themes I have written out, how can I embody these things more every day? What is one thing I can SPEND MONEY on every week that helps me honor myself with these themes in mind?

_____
_____
_____
_____
_____
_____
_____
_____
_____
_____
_____
_____
_____
_____
_____
_____
_____
_____
_____

Day Eleven

Go back and read the list from Day 9. Journal on the following questions:

How could believing only these things about money change my life?

How could I allow myself to believe these things more every day?

_____

_____

_____

_____

_____

_____

_____

_____

_____

_____

_____

_____

_____

_____

_____

_____

_____

_____

_____

_____

_____

_____

_____

_____

Day Twelve

Time to shift again! Write out the following memory. Just like that first memory, it should be detailed, talk about the environment, the lead up, the smells, the people, the feelings.

Describe how it felt when you got your first paycheck, money that you earned, money that was all yours.

How old were you?
What were you doing?
Describe the scene in detail.
Who was with you?
What time of year was it?

_____
_____
_____
_____
_____
_____
_____
_____
_____
_____
_____
_____
_____
_____
_____
_____
_____
_____
_____
_____
_____
_____
_____
_____
_____

Day Thirteen

Go back through days 1-12, read every single journal entry up until now. What observations can you make about money in your life up until now?

How well have your financial decisions reflected those money beliefs you decided you want to have?

What 3 changes can you make to live those beliefs even more?

What else do you feel compelled to write about your money experiences up until now?

_____
_____
_____
_____
_____
_____
_____
_____
_____
_____
_____
_____
_____
_____
_____
_____
_____
_____
_____
_____
_____
_____
_____
_____

Day Fourteen

Today it is important to start with a clear and fresh mind. Take 5 minutes of stillness and quiet before you prepare to write anything.

Now, describe in detail your first negative money memory. The first time thinking about money didn't make you happy.

Be as detailed as possible. Really remember the scene, how did you feel?

How old were you?
What were you doing?
Who was with you?
What time of year was it?

_____
_____
_____
_____
_____
_____
_____
_____
_____
_____
_____
_____
_____
_____
_____
_____
_____
_____
_____
_____
_____

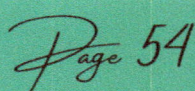

Day Fifteen

Start the day with another 5 minute meditative silence.

Read Day 13 and Day 14.

Without going back to your list of 25, write out every money belief that no longer serves you that you currently have. (A big one for me was "I work hard for my money.")

_____
_____
_____
_____
_____
_____
_____
_____
_____
_____
_____
_____
_____
_____
_____
_____
_____
_____
_____
_____
_____
_____
_____
_____
_____

Day Sixteen

Start the day with another 5 minute meditative silence.

Read day 15 – Do you have anything to add to the list?
Go through every belief and write out how that belief once served you, why it no longer does, and finish with "I am ready to release this belief."

Read each one out loud.

_____
_____
_____
_____
_____
_____
_____
_____
_____
_____
_____
_____
_____
_____
_____
_____
_____
_____
_____
_____
_____
_____
_____
_____
_____
_____

Day Seventeen

Go through the list from Day 16.

Write out each belief again along with the serve / limit and release statement for each. At the end write what you choose to believe instead.

It should read "I choose to believe...."

Read each one out loud.

_____
_____
_____
_____
_____
_____
_____
_____
_____
_____
_____
_____
_____
_____
_____
_____
_____
_____
_____
_____
_____
_____
_____
_____
_____
_____
_____

Day Eighteen

Journal on the following questions. Free write without censoring yourself. Include every thought that comes in.

How have my past money experiences impacted the way I think and feel about money today?

How have these things influenced my financial decisions up until now?

For both of these try to give specific examples of habits, decisions, experiences, etc. The more detailed you are the better.

Day Nineteen

Read all of your past journal entries. As you go, take the time to reflect and add any notes that come to mind.

Now that you have read 18 days of money memories, beliefs and experiences, how do you feel about everything you have written?

Be honest. Include the good, the bad, the ugly.

What have you learned about yourself and your money story?

How do the following scenarios make you feel? Describe why in detail.

Paying bills
Seeing your checking account go under $100
Not having savings
Having Credit Card Debt

Investing in yourself ($5k or more)
Investing in your business ($5k or more)

Seeing $10k in your savings account
Going on your dream vacation?
Hitting your retirement funds goal?

How can you lean even more into abundant thinking for each one of these.

_____
_____
_____
_____
_____
_____
_____
_____
_____
_____
_____
_____
_____
_____
_____
_____
_____
_____
_____
_____

Day Twenty-one

Start with a 10 minute meditation.
Read every entry all the way through.
Allow time to reflect on each day's entry.

Summarize your entire money story as you see it. There are
no rules and no format. This is your story and you get to
tell it how you want.

_____
_____
_____
_____
_____
_____
_____
_____
_____
_____
_____
_____
_____
_____
_____
_____
_____
_____
_____
_____
_____
_____
_____
_____
_____
_____
_____
_____

Now that you have begun to really understand the why's around your relationship with money and have dug even deeper into the memories and experiences that have created those whys, how do you feel about it?

How have these beliefs served you in the past, are they still serving you now? How can you use this knowledge in your wealth building decisions?

CHAPTER THREE
UNDERSTANDING YOUR TRIGGERS

Breaking down the "whys" around our money behaviors is so important, and, as we discussed in previous chapters, often holds the keys to change. That being said, the why isn't the only thing we need to understand and truth be told, probably not the most important for day to day awareness.

In this chapter we are going to talk about triggers... I know, I know, I am not a huge fan of that word either but hear me out. There are things that happen in our lives that prompt an automatic response. Marketers know this and feed on this to get us to buy things that are not in alignment with our goals. These things are called Spending Triggers. Knowing what yours are and creating a system to guide you through is the best way to keep yourself from veering off the path you want to be on.

Scan me

DANGER ZONES AND LIGHTHOUSES

This concept can be broken into 3 simple steps.

1. Identify the things you feel like you spent money on that you maybe wish you didn't. There is almost always a pattern in this type of buying behavior. This pattern is called the Danger Zone.

2. Identify what emotion or experience prompted the purchase. This is called a Spending Trigger. The trigger is typically caused by the type of buyer you are, there are 7 primary types. *These are covered in detail in the training linked on the previous page.*

Everyone is a combination of more than one buying style. How those styles play out as spending triggers are linked to our individual money stories and core values.

All of that being said, each individual purchase is tied to an individual trigger and style and is linked to the danger zone pattern. Identifying what trigger prompted the purchase can be very helpful for the final step.

3. Create a guideline to remind yourself to ask better questions next time (lighthouse). This guideline is typically very action oriented and the purpose is to cause pause and help you stay mindful in your purchase decisions.

Let's look at some examples.

You are scrolling Facebook and see an ad for a super cute shirt.

You click through and buy the shirt.

When you get it, the quality is garbage and even though it was cheap you still would have rather not bought it to begin with.

You would like to say this is the only time this has happened but you know that you get caught up by clever marketing (especially for cute clothes) more than you would like.

This awareness of a pattern is key! As soon as a pattern comes up we can create a lighthouse to guide you through in the future.

**Item Purchased: The Shirt
Spending Trigger: Impulse Buyer
(Refer to videos for more details)**

The clever marker of Facebook has used the knowledge of your love for clothes to create FOMO and get you to buy the shirt without you asking yourself if you really want it or if it will be a good buy.

Lets break this down even further...

Where did you fall out of alignment?

The issue isn't that you bought the shirt, had it been of excellent quality you would not have regretted the purchase at all.

Knowing this, you also know that your lighthouse doesn't need to keep you from buying the shirt, it simply needs to remind you to ask questions and ensure you are buying what you think you are buying.

Misalignment actually occurred when the item you purchased was garbage. Create a Lighthouse or guideline from this place.

For example, if you commit to taking pause and reading reviews of each product before deciding to buy, you are able to confirm you are buying what you think you are buying and give you a chance to change your mind.

Lighthouse:
I promise myself that I will read at least 5 reviews of any item before I purchase it.

 PRACTICE

In the space provided, write out 5 items you have purchased in the past 90 days that were not in alignment with your goals.

Feel free to go through your bank account if it helps you. Identify the Spending Trigger and the lighthouse you are committed to create for yourself.

In the reflections section write out how you will use the money instead. Will you buy something else, pay off debt, save, do something fun? There is no right or wrong answer, just be sure you are choosing from a place of what you really want and not what you think you should do!

Danger Zone	Spending Trigger	Lighthouse

Reflection:

_____

_____

_____

_____

_____

_____

_____

Danger Zone	Spending Trigger	Lighthouse

Reflection:

_____
_____
_____
_____
_____
_____
_____

Danger Zone	Spending Trigger	Lighthouse

Reflection:

_____
_____
_____
_____
_____
_____

Danger Zone	Spending Trigger	Lighthouse

Reflection:

Danger Zone	Spending Trigger	Lighthouse

Reflection:

WHERE DO WE GO FROM HERE?

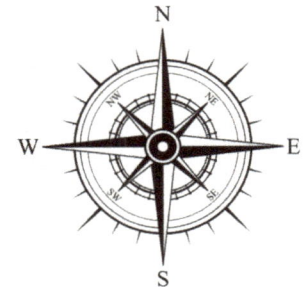

You have done so much work as you have gone through this journal I hope you are proud of yourself! Digging into the "why" behind our actions, thoughts and feelings isn't always easy. Now that you have a better understanding of your relationship with money, your money story and your purchasing patterns you are perfectly equipped to decide where you go from here!

Use the following reflection pages to do exactly that, reflect!

What did you learn about yourself that you didn't know before?

How in alignment with the life you want to live is your spending?

Go back and read your entries, how will this change the way you spend and save in the future?

The choice is yours, I hope you choose happiness and abundance!

-Charissa

About The Author

Charissa Turnbull is an intuitive financial coach, real estate expert and published author.

She helps generous, purpose driven entrepreneurs build wealth without sacrificing their values or their desires using intuitive mapping techniques that encourage creativity and resourcefulness.

Charissa's clients desire to live their lives from a place of joy and happiness while learning to make decisions with ease.

Life is about connections, relationships and experiences! She teaches the best way to live this way without stress, fear or guilt. simply align your money with the life you want to live, not the other way around!

Let's Connect

www.ingramcontent.com/pod-product-compliance
Lightning Source LLC
Chambersburg PA
CBHW051545120626
46551CB00013B/1372